Günter Gerngross
Herbert Puchta

Join us for English

Activity Book Starter

Contents

ELI
CAMBRIDGE UNIVERSITY PRESS

1 Hello!

1 Stick (page 57). Colour and write.

2 Stick (page 57). Colour.

3 Colour and write the names.

1

_ _ _ _

2

_ _ _

3

_ _ _ _

4

_ _ _ _ _

4 Write.

Hello,
I'm Toby.

Hello,
I'm Pat.

Hello,
I'm Mike.

Miaow,
I'm Magic.

5 Listen and tick.

1

☐ yes ☐ no

2

☐ yes ☐ no

3

☐ yes ☐ no

4

☐ yes ☐ no

6 Listen and colour.

1

2

3

4

2 A party

1 Listen and tick.

1

☐ yes ☐ no

2

☐ yes ☐ no

3

☐ yes ☐ no

4

☐ yes ☐ no

2 Match and colour.

three one five

two four six

3 6 2

4

5

1

2 A party

3 Draw.

4 Listen and check.

5 Read the numbers and draw the line.

1	3	4	6	2
5	6	5	4	6
1	2	5	3	6
3	4	6	1	2
5	1	2	3	4

one ↓ three ↓ four ↓ five ↓ five ↓ two ↓ four ↓ six ↓ two ↓ three ↓ four

6 Circle.

2 A party

7 Colour the correct pictures.

1

three frogs

2

two cats

3

five balloons

4

four frogs

5

four balloons

6

six cats

8 **Write and colour.**

three ....

six ....

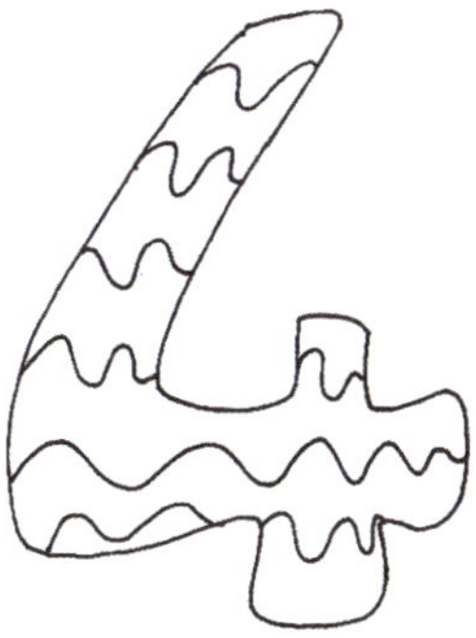

four ....

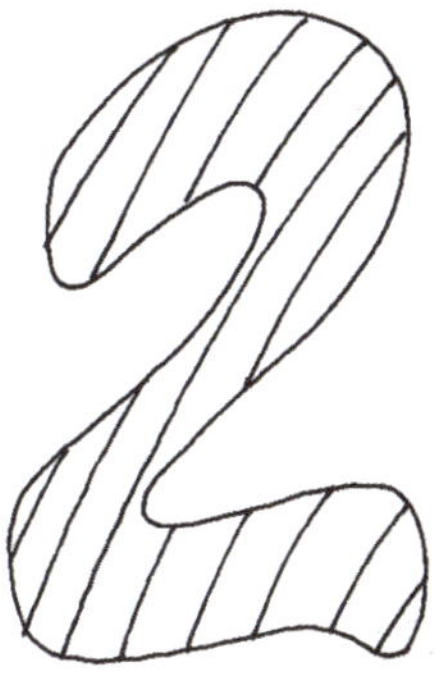

two ....

one ....

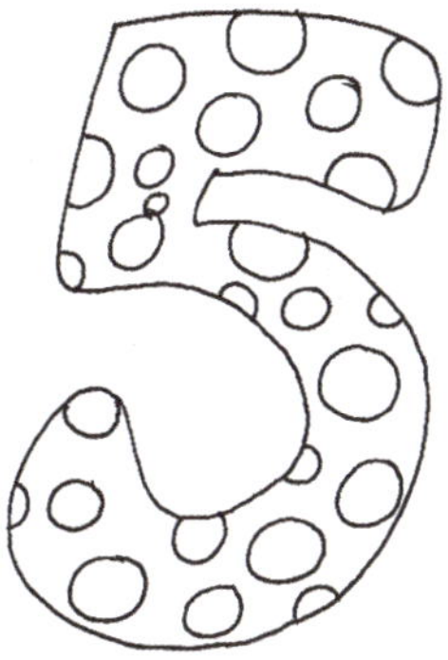

five ....

3 Colours

1 Listen and colour.

2 Colour.

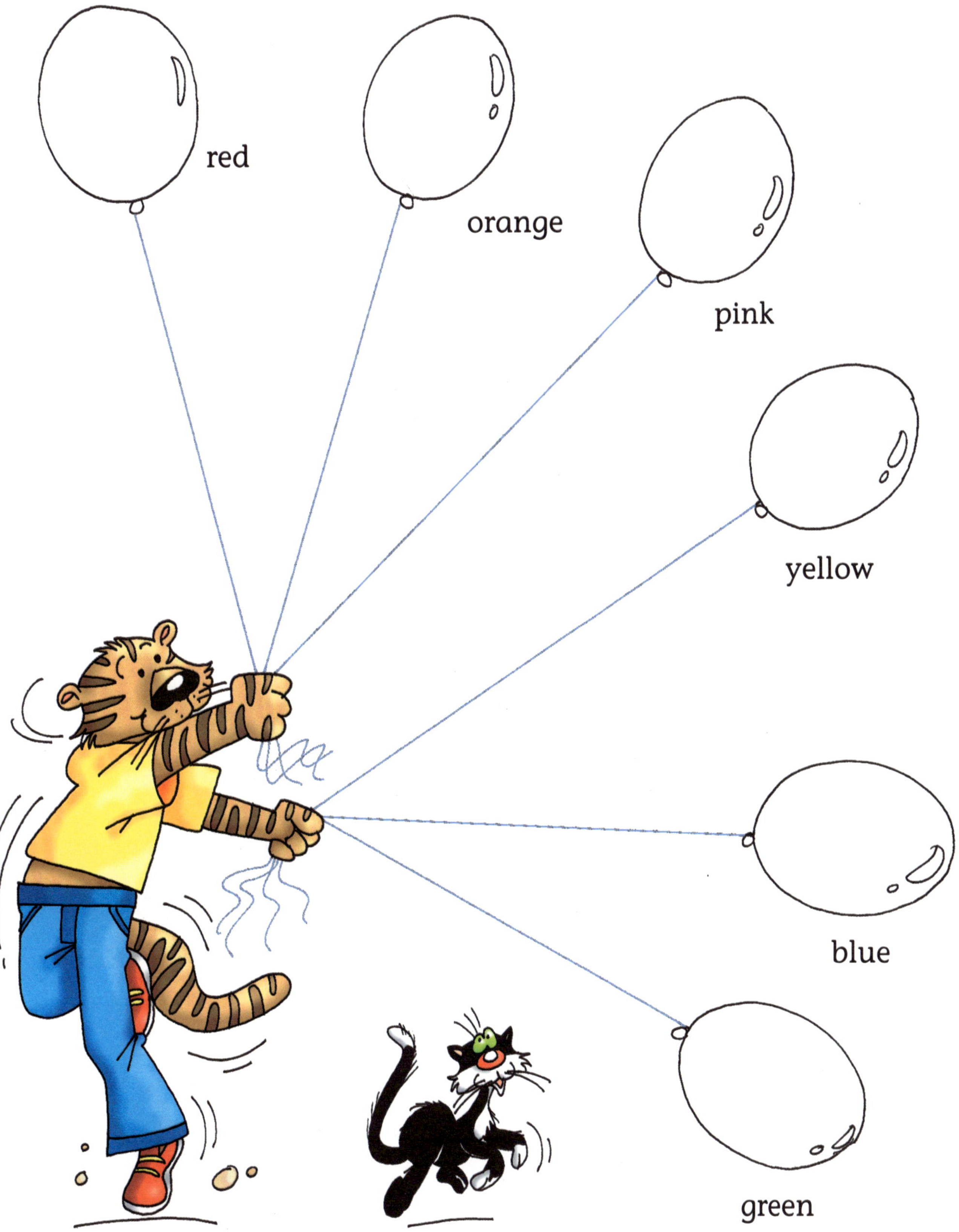

3 Listen and colour.

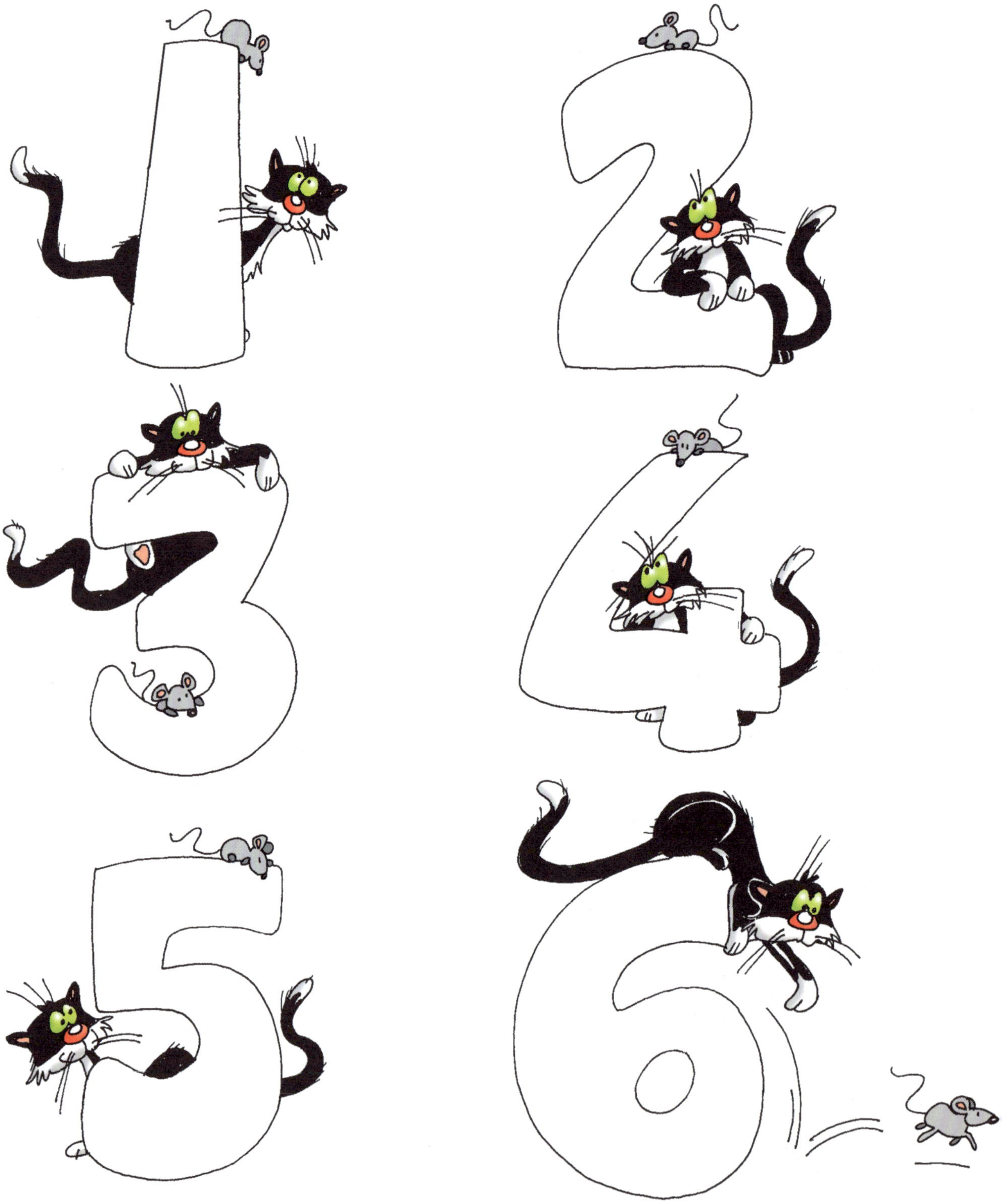

4 Colour.

six red frogs

four pink frogs

five orange frogs

two blue frogs

three yellow frogs

one green frog

1

2

3

4

5

6

5 Colour the British flag.

one = red two = blue

6 Draw and colour your flag.

7 Write. Colour the balloons.

4 School

1 Listen and colour.

2 Count and write.

1 six rubbers

2 books

3 pen

4 bags

5 pencil cases

6 pencils

3 Listen, read and stick (page 59).

1

The bell.

2

Put your books in your bag.

3

Take your bag.

4

Say bye-bye.

4 Listen and match.

5 Write the numbers. Listen and check.

1	3	5	1	3	5	1			
2	4		8						
3	2	1	3	2	1	3			
1	2	3	4	5	4	3			
10	9	8	7	6					
1	10	2	9						

6 Stick (page 63). Listen and check.

$7 + 3 =$ ____

$1 + 8 =$ ____

$2 + 5 =$ ____

$3 + 2 =$ ____

$4 + 2 =$ ____

$5 + 3 =$ ____

7 **Listen and write the numbers.**

1 Circle the words.

2 Find the colours.

1. iknp _ _ _ _
2. wllyoe _ _ _ _ _ _
3. dre _ _ _
4. lbeu _ _ _ _
5. reogan _ _ _ _ _ _
6. ergen _ _ _ _ _

3 Listen and colour.

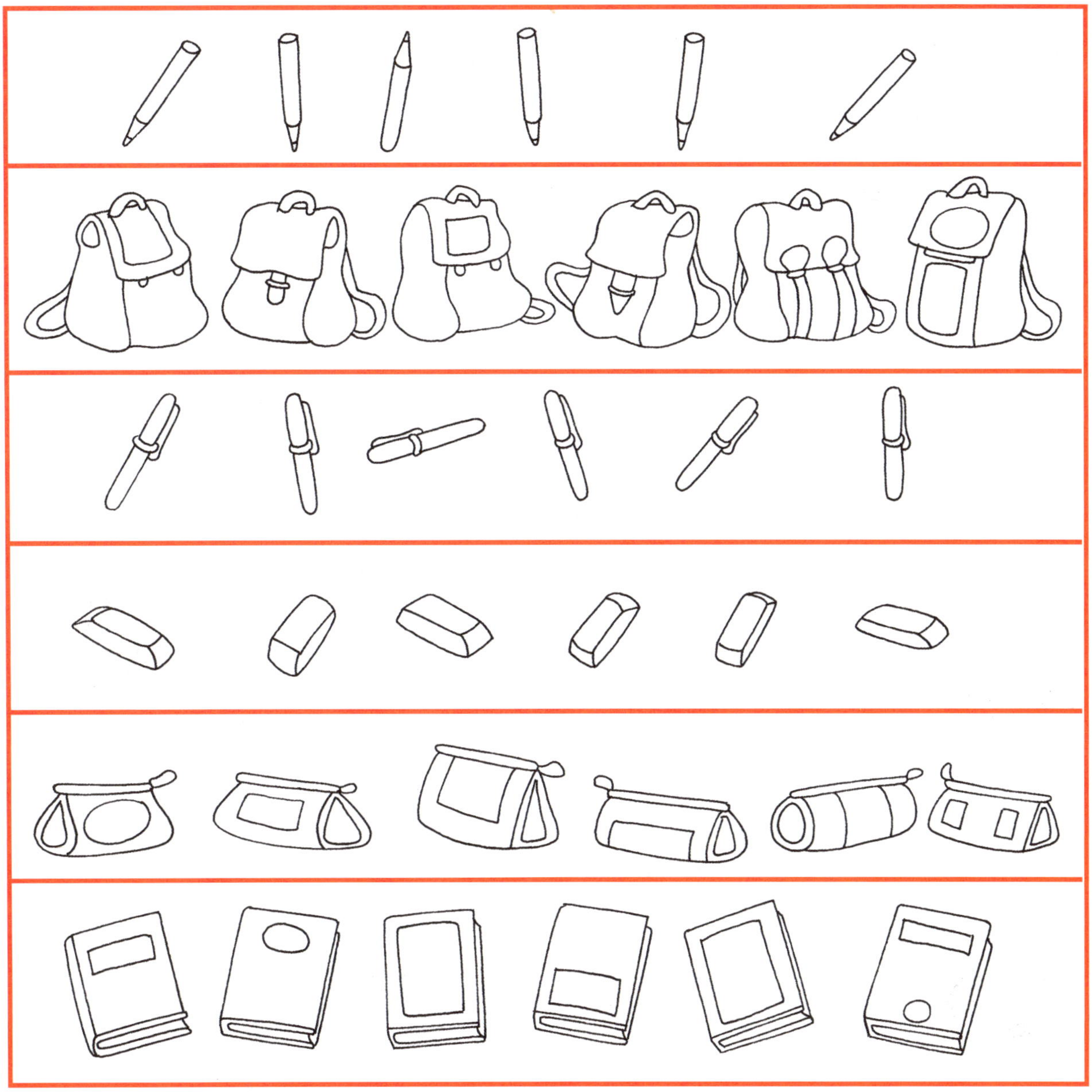

4 Complete.

1. Two red pencils.
2. .... orange ....
3. Six .... pens.
4. .... pink ....
5. Three green ....
6. Four .... books.

5 Animals

1 Write the numbers. Listen and check.

one	two
three	four
five	six
seven	eight
nine	ten

2 Listen and tick.

1

☐ yes ☐ no

2

☐ yes ☐ no

3

☐ yes ☐ no

4

☐ yes ☐ no

3 Match.

1 

one mouse

2 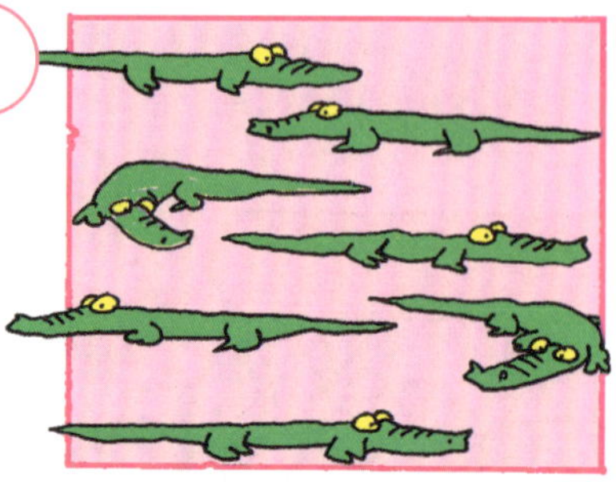

seven crocodiles

3 

ten books

4 

nine frogs

5 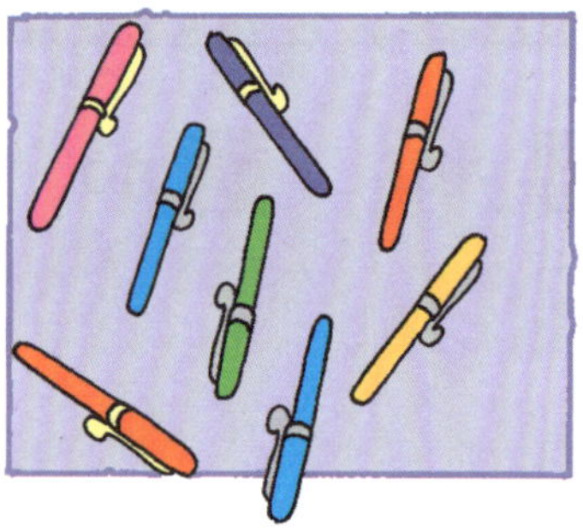

eight pens

6 

six pencils

7 

five lions

8 

three pencil cases

9 

four balloons

10 

two bags

4 Tick.

1

seven lions ☐ yes ☐ no

2

nine crocodiles ☐ yes ☐ no

3

eight cats ☐ yes ☐ no

4

seven frogs ☐ yes ☐ no

5 Circle the words. Write.

6 Read and colour.

one orange lion

six blue frogs

two yellow lions

ten red elephants

eight red frogs

nine green cats

four blue crocodiles

five pink cats

6 Party food

1 Listen and stick (page 63).

1

2

3

4

5

6

2 Read and colour.

1

2

lollipops

apples

chocolate

ice cream

popcorn

oranges

bananas

3

4

5

6

7

3 Listen and tick.

1

☐ yes ☐ no

2

☐ yes ☐ no

3

☐ yes ☐ no

4

☐ yes ☐ no

4 Match.

1 

chocolate

2 

apples

3 

lollipops

4 

ice cream

5 

popcorn

6 

oranges

7 

bananas

5 Draw.

6 Listen and check.

7 Write the words.

1 Listen and tick.

1

2

3

4

5

6

2 Read and stick (page 63).

two apples

five oranges

chocolate

seven lollipops

ice cream

three bananas

3 Complete.

1. elephant • elephant • lion • lion • elephant • elephant • lion • ....
2. frog • cat • cat • frog • cat • cat • frog • .... • ....
3. mouse • crocodile • lion • mouse • crocodile • ....
4. cat • cat • lion • lion • mouse • cat • cat • lion • .... • ....
5. crocodile • crocodile • frog • lion • crocodile • .... • .... • lion

4 Listen and check.

7 Let's play!

1 Look and count.

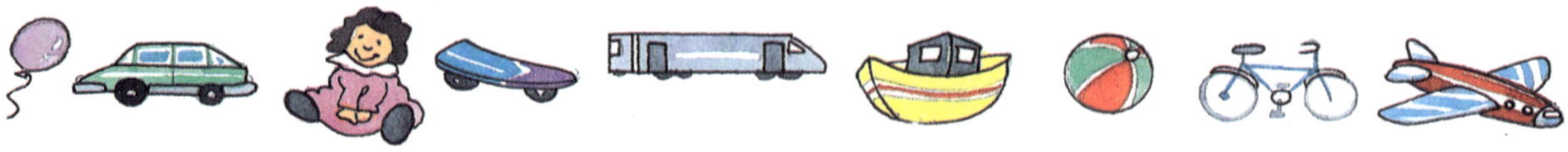

6

2 Listen and check.

3 Look and count.

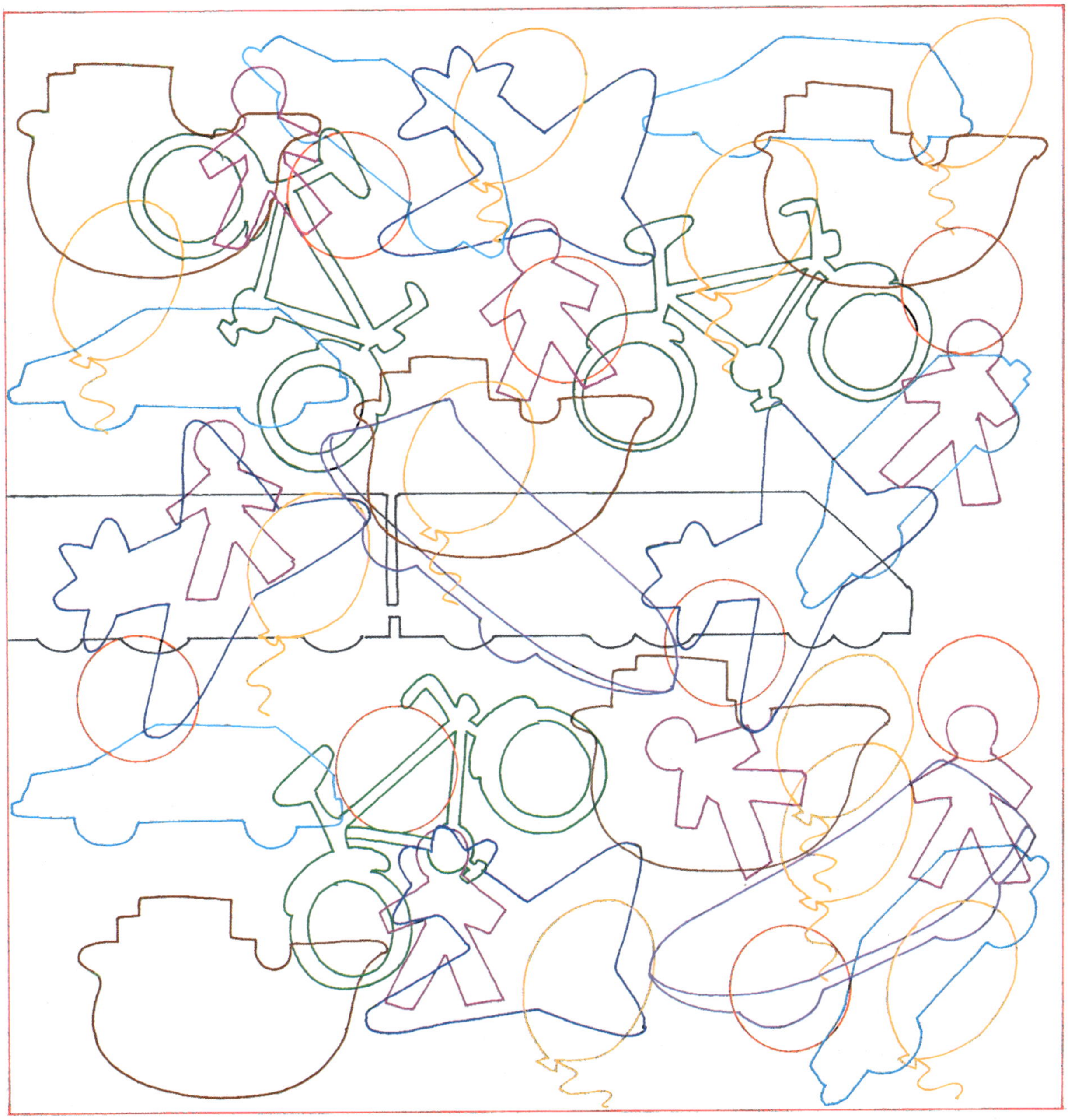

7								

4 Listen and check.

5 Match and write.

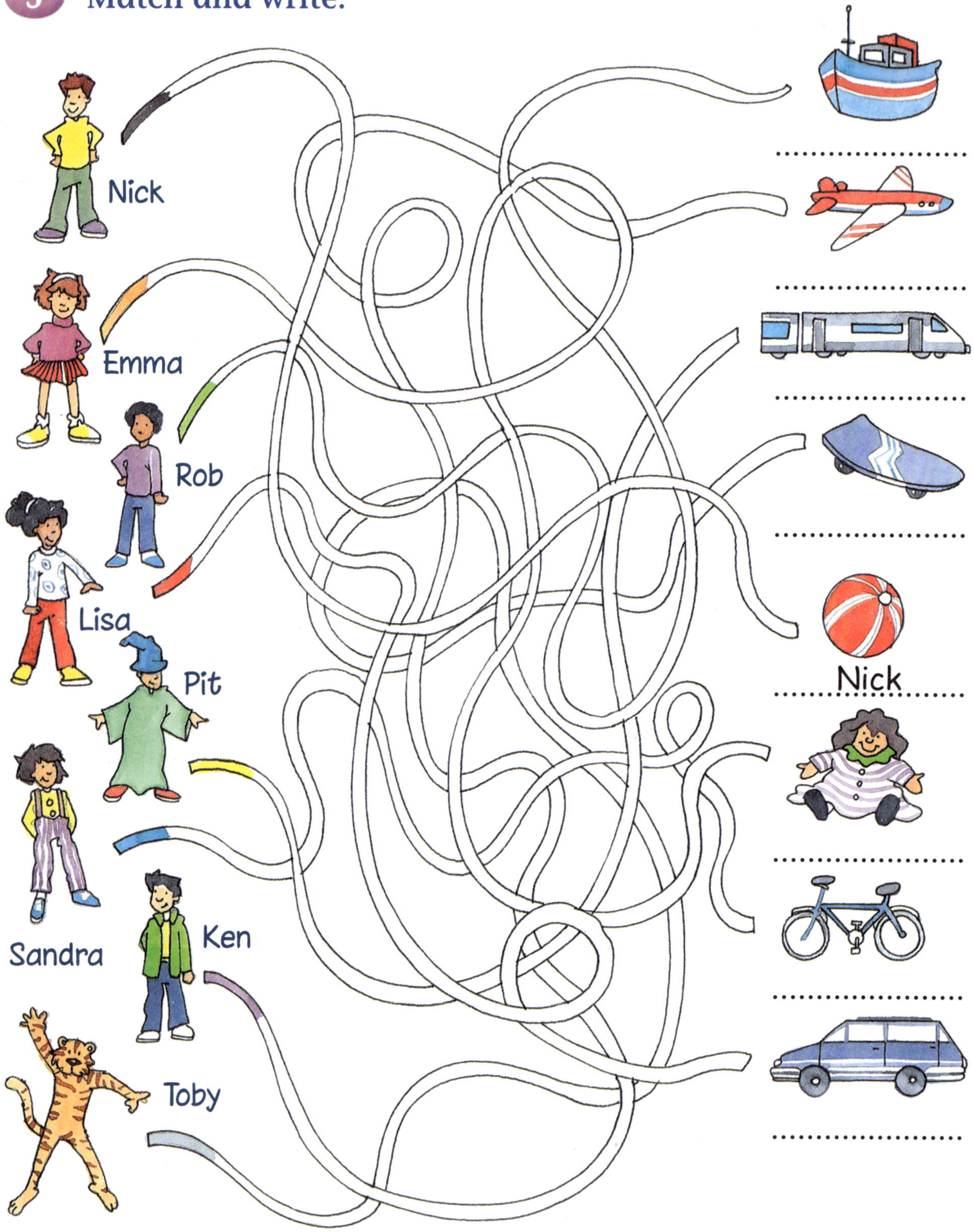

6 Listen and check.

7 Read and match.

1

2

bike

boat

skateboard

doll

plane

ball

3

4

5

6

8 Listen and tick.

1

☐ yes ☐ no

2

☐ yes ☐ no

3

☐ yes ☐ no

4

☐ yes ☐ no

9 Write.

1

_ _ _ _ _

2

_ _ _ _

3

_ _ _ _

4

_ _ _ _ _ _ _ _ _ _

5

_ _ _

6

_ _ _ _

7

_ _ _ _ _

8

_ _ _ _

8 Holidays

1 Join the numbers.

five

four • six

three • seven

two • eight

• nine

one • ten

2 Colour.

1 red	3 green	5 yellow
2 orange	4 blue	6 pink

3 Read and match.

1

2

3

4

Let's play!

Let's go to the beach!

Ice cream... yummy!

Let's swim!

4 Listen, read and stick (page 61).

1

Go to the beach.

2

Jump.

3

Ouch!

4

It's a crab.

5 Listen and tick.

1

☐ yes ☐ no

2

☐ yes ☐ no

3

☐ yes ☐ no

4

☐ yes ☐ no

6 **Complete.**

Let's | the beach | Ice cream | play

Revision 3

1 Read, draw and colour.

two yellow cats

five blue crocodiles

six pink elephants

three orange frogs

2 Complete.

Number one is ....red..........

Number two is ....

Number three is ....

Number four is ....

Number five is ....

Number six is ....

3 Colour. Count and write.

1 one .... bag.

2 four ....

3 two ....

4 six ....

5 three ....

6 seven ....

4 Circle the words. Write.

Cutouts

page 2

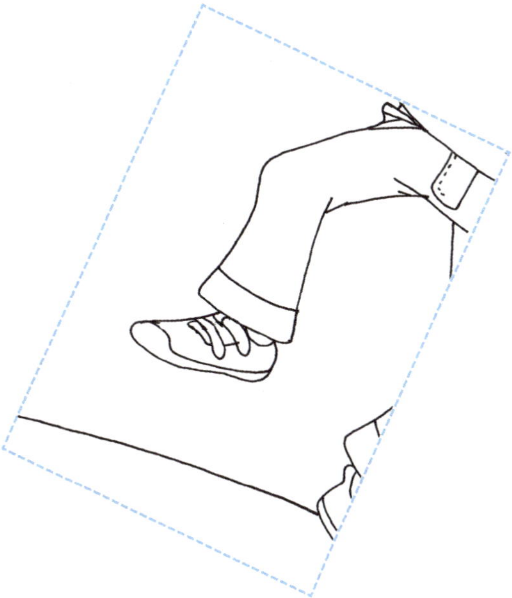

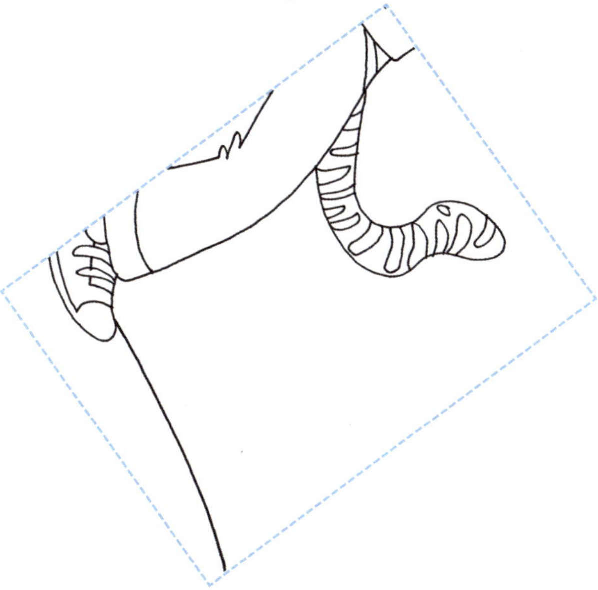

page 3

Toby	Emma	Mike
Magic	Pit	Pat

page 22

page 51

Cutouts

page 24

ten	seven	nine
six	five	eight

page 34

page 41